Pronunciation Pairworks

PronPack 3
Pronunciation Pairworks

- A four-book set for teachers of English
- Fun-packed pronunciation activities
- Easy-to-follow presentation notes
- Extra resources on PronPack.com
- Print-friendly worksheets

By Mark Hancock

Hancock McDonald
ENGLISH LANGUAGE TEACHING

PronPack 3 Pronunciation Pairworks

By Mark Hancock

Published by **Hancock McDonald ELT**
Chester. CH1 2AW UK
www.hancockmcdonald.com

First Published 2017

ISBN: 978-0-9957575-3-0

Contents

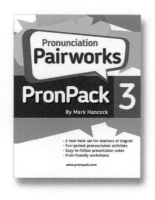

PronPack 3: Pronunciation Pairworks

PronPack 3: Activities and Worksheets

End Matter

Introduction

The Book

What is PronPack?

PronPack is a set of four resource books to help teachers focus on English pronunciation in class. The books contain printable worksheets along with teacher's notes explaining how to use them. Each of the four books takes a slightly different approach to pronunciation teaching. You can select the approach you prefer, or use the various books to complement one another.

What are Pronunciation Pairworks?

Pronunciation Pairworks are information-gap communication activities for students to do in pairs or small groups. Success in each activity depends upon the students accurately producing and understanding the target pronunciation feature.

What are the benefits of doing these pairworks?

The pairworks can benefit learners by forcing them to focus on the accuracy of their production and understanding of hard-to-distinguish features of English pronunciation. Failure to produce or perceive the difference sufficiently will mean failure to complete the activity. A further benefit of the pairworks is that they show how the pronunciation feature in question is important to meaning and intelligibility – too often, students get the impression that pronunciation is merely about sounding good.

What aspects of pronunciation are covered?

The pairworks at the beginning of the book focus on individual sounds, usually through minimal pairs. The minimal pairs are contextualized as names on maps, sentence pairs, picture descriptions or games. The pairworks later in the book focus on word stress, tonic stress and phrasal homophones.

What are the other books in the PronPack collection?

The other three books in the series are:

PronPack 1: Pronunciation Workouts – extended choral drill activities.

PronPack 2: Pronunciation Puzzles – puzzles and game-like activities.

PronPack 4: Pronunciation Poems – poems, raps and chants.

The Approach

Why teach pronunciation?

The most important reason to teach pronunciation is to help your students understand and be understood. As listeners, they need to learn how other speakers blend sounds into words and words into connected speech. As speakers, they need to modify their own accent of English to make it as widely intelligible as possible. Neither of these objectives requires them to precisely copy the accent of a native speaker. The aim is successful communication, not 'correctness'.

What is the pronunciation model?

In the context of your classroom, the best pronunciation model is almost certainly you, the teacher. PronPack aims to be as flexible as possible – you should be able to work with it whether your own accent is from London or Sydney, Turkey or Argentina. Although the phonemic symbols used are based on a British model, they are not intended to be prescriptive. For instance, /e/ does not specify the precise quality of the vowel, but merely that it is different from /æ/ or /ɪ/.

Do I have to know the phonemic alphabet?

You don't have to know or use the phonemic alphabet for the pairworks. Phonemic symbols are sometimes used as titles for different versions of the activity, but the activity does not depend on the student knowing them.

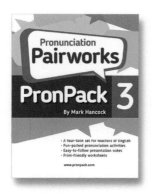

Do these activities work only for one accent?

The material does not restrict you to teaching towards a specific accent. For instance, the activities don't prescribe the **silent r** in words like *hair*, *arm*, *fork* and *bird*. It is optional, and is shown in brackets in the **PronPack Sound Chart**. If you choose to model the pairworks yourself and you have an accent where the **silent r** is pronounced, they still work fine. However, the audio files, if you choose to use them, are recorded in a General British accent. Note that there is both a British and an American version of the **PronPack Sound Chart**.

Note that the symbols which appear between slanted brackets in this book, such as /ʌ/ or /ʃ/, are strictly speaking, phonemes rather than sounds. A phoneme such as /ʌ/ corresponds to slightly different sounds across different accents.

Flexi notes throughout the books highlight ways that you can adapt the material to work with different accents.

The Activities

What materials are in the book?

The book contains printable worksheets for the students and teacher's notes for you. The teacher's notes highlight the teaching focus, minimum student level, and indicate printing requirements and audio files for each activity. The notes give a short background to the pronunciation point plus-a-step by step procedure for using the activity in class.

How long do the activities take?

Each activity will typically take around 15-20 minutes of class time, although this can vary a lot depending on how thoroughly you exploit the material. If you would like to spend longer, you can combine the *pairworks* with a *workout*, *puzzle* or *poem* focusing on the same pronunciation point from **PronPack 1, 2** or **4**. Recommended combinations are given in the *Lesson Plans* section, page 10 and in the **Goes well with ...** notes at the end of each activity.

Do I have to print out the worksheets?

The worksheets in **Pronunciation Pairworks** can be printed out, or alternatively, you could project them. However, for some of the activities, it is better if the student has their own printed copy because they may need to write on the sheet or follow a route on the map.

What level are the activities designed for?

The minimum level is indicated in the teacher's notes for each pairwork, but remember that this is a minimum level. An activity which is suitable for a pre-intermediate learner can be just as valuable for an upper intermediate learner – pronunciation often lags behind other competences because it has been neglected.

Are the activities for a specific age group or class size?

The activities are not aimed at a specific age group and should benefit young learners and adults alike. As they are pairworks you will need at least two students in your class unless you participate in the activity yourself. If you have an odd number of students, you can adapt the activities for groups of three.

What are the audio files for?

There are audio files for some of the lessons. Teachers can use these if they are not confident about their own pronunciation. However, you can model the pairworks yourself instead of using the audio files, and this is usually the better option. You could use the audio to guide you in this rehearsal.

The Website

What will I find on the support website?

PronPack.com provides additional information for users of **PronPack** including downloadable poster versions of the *PronPack Sound Charts* and **Free** extra pronunciation activities.

If you have purchased an ePub or the print-version of this book we would like to thank you for supporting our endeavour. On the website you will have access to teacher resources to accompany the activities including:

- Print-friendly PDF files of the activity worksheets

- Slides to use during the presentation phase of the lessons

- Downloadable MP3 audio files as required

- Updates and additional materials

Note: The interactive functionality of the fixed-layout ePub will depend on your device and/or the ePub reader available for your device.

Contact us

We'd welcome your feedback on www.pronpack.com and invite you to share your thoughts and reactions on the book seller's website.

Please get in touch with us through our website if you have any difficulties with the material or would like to make a suggestion for another activity.

Connect with us on:

 twitter.com/pronpackbooks (@pronpackbooks)

facebook.com/pronpack

Lesson Plans

If you plan to focus on a particular pronunciation point, here are some recommended activity combinations from across the **PronPack Collection** (books **1**, **2**, **3** and **4**):

- **Awareness of sounds: 2.1** and **2.6**
- **The complete sound system: 1.1, 1.2** and **1.3**
- **Long versus short vowels: 3.1** Version 1, **3.2** Version 2 and **4.1**
- **The *R* vowels: 1.4, 2.2** Version 4 and **4.3**
- **Vowels spelt with 2 letters: 1.5, 2.12, 2.2** Version 5 and **4.4**
- **Short vowels: 1.6, 2.3, 3.1** Version 2, **3.3** vowel pairs and **4.2**
- **Stop consonants: 1.7, 3.4** Version 1, **3.3** consonant pairs and **4.11**
- **Fricatives and affricates: 1.8, 2.2** Version 2, **3.4** Version 3, **4.9** and **4.10**
- **Semi-vowels: 2.2** Version 3, **3.4** Version 2 and **4.7**
- **/l/ versus /r/: 3.2** Version 3, **3.5** Version 3 and **4.8**
- **Consonant clusters: 1.9** and **4.13**
- **-ed endings: 2.2** Version 6 and **4.14**
- **/s/ versus /z/ and –s endings: 2.2** Version 1, **3.5** Version 2 and **4.15**
- **Word stress: 2.9** and **3.6**
- **Word stress families: 1.10, 2.7, 3.8** and **4.16**
- **Weak forms: 1.11, 2.4** Version 2, **4.5** and **4.17**
- **Rhythm: 1.12** and **4.16**
- **Tonic stress: 1.13, 2.9, 3.10, 3.11** and **3.12**
- **Connected speech: 2.5, 2.10** and **3.9**

Goes well with ...

... These combinations are also given at the end of each activity.

Map of the Book

The PronPack Sound Chart	A teaching and reference tool for the individual sounds of English, including an explanatory Infographic. This book has two versions of the Chart: **IPA** with guidewords and **American** with guidewords.		
PAIRWORKS	**TEACHING FOCUS**	**MINIMUM LEVEL**	**ACTIVITY**
3.1 Air Traffic Control	Minimal pairs:/iː ɪ/; /e æ/; /eə ɪə/; /aʊ uː/	Pre-intermediate	Giving and following a route on a grid
3.2 Hear Say Dominoes	Minimal pairs: **Version 1:** /p b/; /t d/; /k g/; **Version 2:** /ɪ iː/; /e eɪ/; /ɒ əʊ/; **Version 3:** /r//l/	Pre-intermediate	A minimal pair discrimination game
3.3 West or East	Minimal pairs:/p b/; /b v/; /f v/; /s z/; /r l/; /t d/; /ɪ iː/; /e eɪ/; /ɒ əʊ/; /æ e/; /ɔː əʊ/; /æ ʌ/	Pre-intermediate	A minimal pair discrimination game
3.4 Street Maps	Minimal pairs: **Version 1:** /b v/; /b p/; /k g/; /m n/; **Version 2:** /d t/; /s θ/; /v w/; /z ð/; **Version 3:** /s ʃ/; /t ʃ/; /j dʒ/; /tʃ dʒ/	Pre-intermediate	A minimal pair discrimination game
3.5 Box Sets	Minimal pairs: **Version 1:** /ɪ iː/; /eə ɪə/; /e eɪ/; **Version 2:** /s z/; /ʃ tʃ/; /t d/; **Version 3:** /l r/	Pre-intermediate	A minimal pair discrimination game
3.6 Syllable Dice	Stress in words and phrases relating to time and number	Elementary	A dice and grid game
3.7 One Stress or Two?	Stress in compound nouns	Intermediate	A stress minimal pair discrimination game
3.8 Stress Pinball	Stress pattern changes with noun and verb	Intermediate	A stress minimal pair discrimination game
3.9 Sound Bites	Phrasal homophones	Pre-intermediate	A listen-and-find game
3.10 Eye Witness	Tonic stress placement for given and new information	Pre-intermediate	Interview role-play
3.11 Response Questions	Tonic stress placement for contrast	Intermediate	Interview role-play
3.12 Contrastive Shapes	Contrastive stress	Pre-intermediate	Guessing game

The PronPack Sound Chart

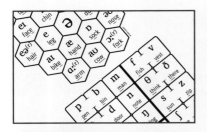

PRONPACK SOUND CHARTS

PronPack Infographic
PronPack Sound Chart 1
PronPack Sound Chart 2

What is the Sound Chart for?

Reference

The *PronPack Sound Chart* is primarily a reference tool. Teachers can print a copy as large as possible to put on the classroom wall. Whenever a pronunciation point comes up in class relating to one or more of the individual sounds, you can point it out on the chart.

Over time, the class will become more and more familiar with it. However, to get students started with the chart, you may want to devote some class time to presenting and exploring it more intensively. There are lessons focusing on the chart in **PronPack 1: Pronunciation Workouts**.

Orientation

The *PronPack Sound Chart* is intended to help you and the class find your way around the sounds of English. It enables you to see the 'big picture' – the entire system – at a glance. This is useful because if you just encounter the sounds one by one, you have no idea of where you are in the system as a whole. It could appear limitless and consequently impossible to master.

Comparison

The *PronPack Sound Chart* graphically represents relationships between the sounds, showing those that are comparable with each other and those which are very different. This helps to promote an understanding of the whole system, as well as making it more memorable. Regular users will eventually be able to remember which sound occupies which place in the chart as a whole.

How is the Sound Chart organised?

The *PronPack Sound Chart Infogaphic* on page 15 explains how the Sound Chart is organised. This is primarily for you, but you could print it out for your students at the beginning of the course too.

Note: You will find downloadable poster versions of the *PronPack Sound Charts* at www.pronpack.com

Chart 1 IPA Phonemic Symbols with Guide Words

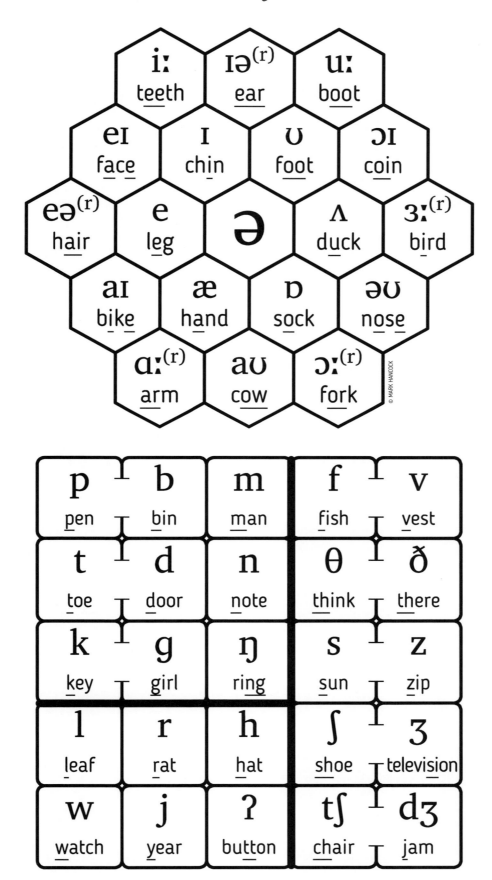

© MARK HANCOCK

Chart 2 American Symbols with Guide Words

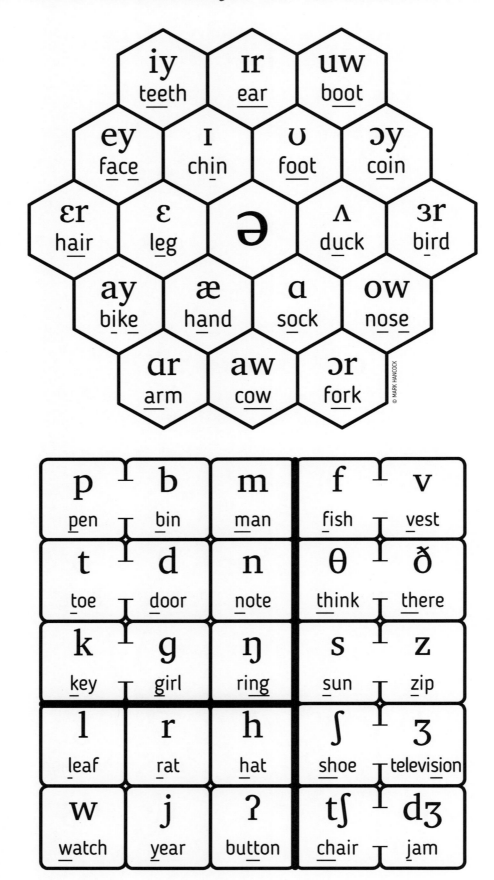

© MARK HANCOCK

PronPack 3 Pronunciation Pairworks: The PronPack Sound Chart   © Mark Hancock 2017

Infographic The PronPack Sound Chart

Vowels
in the hexagon...

Six Long vowels
Symbols usually have **:** but /eə/ also considered a long vowel in this model.

Corners

Outer Circle

Six Diphthongs
Symbols have two elements; the sound moves from one position to the other.

Sides

Six Short vowels
Symbols are all single; these vowels never end a syllable.

Inner Circle

Jaw and lip positions

closed, wide / closed, round
mid – wide / relaxed
open, wide / open, round

The weak vowel
Also known as 'schwa'; only used in unstressed syllables; the most common sound in English!

Centre

Optional r
The letter **r** usually comes after these sounds; pronounced in some accents, not in others.

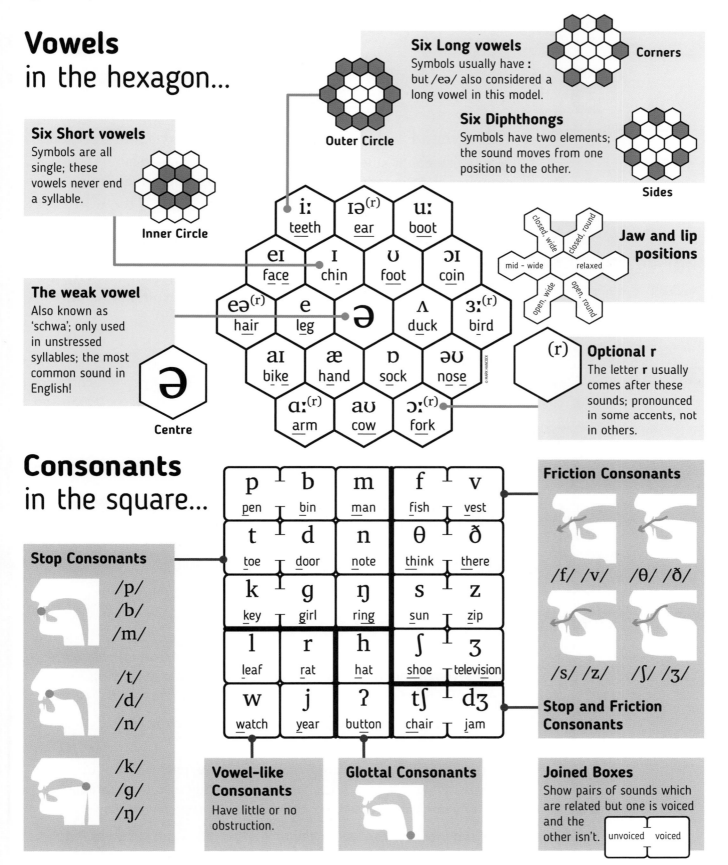

Hexagon chart:

- iː teeth | ɪə(r) ear | uː boot
- eɪ face | ɪ chin | ʊ foot | ɔɪ coin
- eə(r) hair | e leg | ə | ʌ duck | ɜː(r) bird
- aɪ bike | æ hand | ɒ sock | əʊ nose | (r)
- ɑː(r) arm | aʊ cow | ɔː(r) fork

© MARK HANCOCK

Consonants
in the square...

Stop Consonants

/p/
/b/
/m/

/t/
/d/
/n/

/k/
/g/
/ŋ/

p pen	b bin	m man	f fish	v vest
t toe	d door	n note	θ think	ð there
k key	g girl	ŋ ring	s sun	z zip
l leaf	r rat	h hat	ʃ shoe	ʒ television
w watch	j year	ʔ button	tʃ chair	dʒ jam

Vowel-like Consonants
Have little or no obstruction.

Glottal Consonants

Friction Consonants

/f/ /v/   /θ/ /ð/

/s/ /z/   /ʃ/ /ʒ/

Stop and Friction Consonants

Joined Boxes
Show pairs of sounds which are related but one is voiced and the other isn't.

unvoiced   voiced

Air Traffic Control

3.1

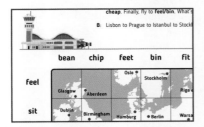

Background

A minimal pair is a pair of words or phrases with identical pronunciation except for one phoneme. For example, the words *bean* and *bin* are identical except for the vowel sound, which is /iː/ for **bean** and /ɪ/ for **bin**. If such a sound difference does not exist in the in the students' first language, they are likely to find it problematic both for understanding and in being understood. The minimal pairs used in this activity are as follows: /iː/ and / ɪ/; /e/ and /æ/; /eə/ and /ɪə/;/aʊ/ and /uː/. There is also an empty version for you to put in your own minimal pairs.

Presentation

1. Draw a 4x4 grid on the board representing the the top left corner of the map and write in the city names, *Glasgow*, *Aberdeen*, *Dublin* and *Birmingham*. Label the columns and rows according to the version you are using, for example *bean* and *chip* and *feel* and *sit* for **Version 1** as shown in **DIAGRAM 3.1A**.

2. Demonstrate how the words can be used as coordinates to refer to one of the squares. For example, if you say *sit - bean*, you are referring to the square containing **Dublin**. If you say *feel - chip*, you are referring to the square containing **Aberdeen**.

3. Get students to practise this in pairs, with one of them saying the coordinate words and the other saying the city names.

Activity

1. Select a version of *Worksheet 3.1*. Point out the example directions at the top of the worksheet and elicit that **Speaker A** is giving a route from the map and **B** is listening and following the route.

2. Now ask students to draw a flight plan connecting four cities on their map without letting their partner see.

3. Students explain their flight plan to their partner without using the names of the airports, following the model in the example conversation at the top of the worksheet, then check answers.

4. Students play this game a number of times using different flight paths and changing partners.

Note: Use the blank map **Version 5**, to practise a different set of minimal pairs of your own selection.

Airport Cities:

Aberdeen /æbəˈdiːn/ UK (Scotland)
Alexandria /ælɪgˈzændriə/ Egypt
Algiers /ælˈdʒɪez/ Algeria
Athens /ˈæθənz/ Greece
Barcelona /bɑːsəˈləʊnə/ Spain (Catalonia)
Belgrade /belˈgreɪd/ Serbia
Benghazi /benˈgɑːzi/ Libya
Berlin /bɜːˈlɪn/ Germany
Birmingham /ˈbɜːmɪŋəm/ UK (England)
Bordeaux /bɔːˈdəʊ/ France
Bucharest /buːkəˈrest/ Romania
Cardiff /ˈkɑːdɪf/ UK (Wales)
Casablanca /kæsəˈblæŋkə/ Morocco
Dublin /ˈdʌblɪn/ Eire (Ireland)
Frankfurt /ˈfræŋkfɜːt/ Germany
Glasgow /ˈglæzgəʊ/ UK (Scotland)
Hamburg /ˈhæmbɜːg/ Germany
Istanbul /ɪstæmˈbʊl/ Turkey
Kiev /kiːˈev/ Ukraine
Krakow /ˈkrækɒv/ Poland
Lisbon /ˈlɪzbən/ Portugal
Milan /mɪˈlæn/ Italy
Minsk /mɪnsk/ Belorussia
Naples /ˈneɪplz/ Italy
Oslo /ˈɒzləʊ/ Norway
Paris /ˈpærɪs/ France
Prague /prɑːg/ Czech Republic
Riga /ˈriːgə/ Latvia
Saint Petersburg /səntˈpiːtəzbɜːg/ Russia
Santiago /sæntiˈɑːgəʊ/ Spain (Galicia)
Sardinia /sɑːˈdɪniə/ (this is an island rather than a city) Italy
Stockholm /ˈstɒkhəʊm/ Sweden
Tripoli /ˈtrɪpəli/ Libya
Tunis /ˈtjuːnɪs/ Tunisia
Warsaw /ˈwɔːsɔː/ Poland
Zagreb /ˈzɑːgreb/ Croatia

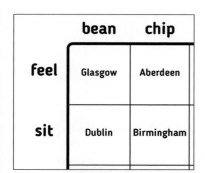

DIAGRAM 3.1A

	bean	chip
feel	Glasgow	Aberdeen
sit	Dublin	Birmingham

MORE IDEAS

If your students are interested in the pronunciation of the airport cities in this game, and the countries where they are located, refer to the **Airport Cities** list on this page.

You could use this information to conduct a class quiz.

3.1 Goes well with...

... **Version 1** goes well with **PronPack 3.2** Version 2 and **PronPack 4.1** for a lesson on long versus short vowels.
... **Version 2** goes well with **PronPack** 1.6, **PronPack 2.3**, **PronPack 3.3** vowel pairs and **PronPack 4.2** for a lesson on short vowels.

/iː/ /ɪ/

Example:

A: Fly from **seat/bean** to **live/bin**. Then fly to **seat/cheap**. Finally, fly to **feel/bin**. What's the flight path?

B: Lisbon to Prague to Istanbul to Stockholm!

	bean	chip	feet	bin	fit	cheap
feel	Glasgow	Aberdeen	Oslo	Stockholm	Riga	Saint Petersburg
sit	Dublin	Birmingham	Hamburg	Berlin	Warsaw	Minsk
live	Cardiff	Paris	Frankfurt	Prague	Krakow	Kiev
fill	Santiago	Bordeaux	Milan	Zagreb	Belgrade	Bucharest
seat	Lisbon	Barcelona	Sardinia	Naples	Athens	Istanbul
leave	Casablanca	Algiers	Tunis	Tripoli	Benghazi	Alexandria

/æ/ /e/

Example:

A: Fly from **dad/bed** to **gas/bad**. Then fly to **dad/men**. Finally, fly to **guess/bad**. What's the flight path?

B: Lisbon to Prague to Istanbul to Stockholm!

	bed	man	sad	bad	said	men
guess	Glasgow	Aberdeen	Oslo	Stockholm	Riga	Saint Petersburg
dead	Dublin	Birmingham	Hamburg	Berlin	Warsaw	Minsk
gas	Cardiff	Paris	Frankfurt	Prague	Krakow	Kiev
sat	Santiago	Bordeaux	Milan	Zagreb	Belgrade	Bucharest
dad	Lisbon	Barcelona	Sardinia	Naples	Athens	Istanbul
sat	Casablanca	Algiers	Tunis	Tripoli	Benghazi	Alexandria

/eə/ /ɪə/

Example:

A: Fly from **bear/fair** to **beer/hear**. Then fly to **bear/hair**. Finally, fly to **air/hear**. What's the flight path?

B: Lisbon to Prague to Istanbul to Stockholm!

	fair	fear	chairs	hear	cheers	hair
air	Glasgow	Aberdeen	Oslo	Stockholm	Riga	Saint Petersburg
dear	Dublin	Birmingham	Hamburg	Berlin	Warsaw	Minsk
beer	Cardiff	Paris	Frankfurt	Prague	Krakow	Kiev
dare	Santiago	Bordeaux	Milan	Zagreb	Belgrade	Bucharest
bear	Lisbon	Barcelona	Sardinia	Naples	Athens	Istanbul
ear	Casablanca	Algiers	Tunis	Tripoli	Benghazi	Alexandria

/əʊ/ /uː/

Example:

A: Fly from **grow/blow** to **grew/toe**. Then fly to **grow/two**. Finally, fly to **show/toe**. What's the flight path?

B: Lisbon to Prague to Istanbul to Stockholm!

	blow	**soup**	**blue**	**toe**	**soap**	**two**
show	Glasgow	Aberdeen	Oslo	Stockholm	Riga	Saint Petersburg
boat	Dublin	Birmingham	Hamburg	Berlin	Warsaw	Minsk
grew	Cardiff	Paris	Frankfurt	Prague	Krakow	Kiev
shoe	Santiago	Bordeaux	Milan	Zagreb	Belgrade	Bucharest
grow	Lisbon	Barcelona	Sardinia	Naples	Athens	Istanbul
boot	Casablanca	Algiers	Tunis	Tripoli	Benghazi	Alexandria

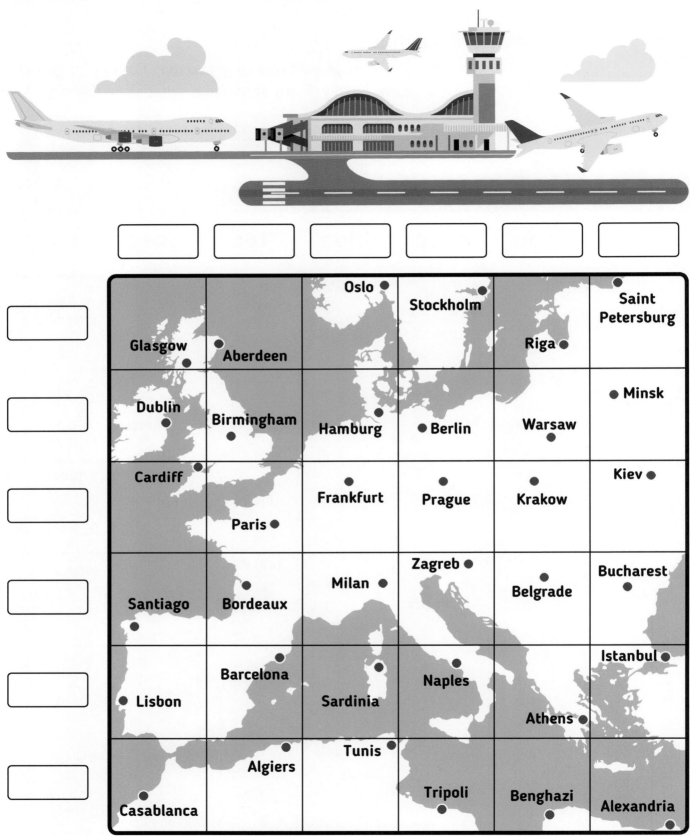

Hear Say Dominoes

3.2

TEACHING FOCUS

To practise perceiving and producing the difference between minimal pairs:
Version 1: /p b/; /t d/; /k g/;
Version 2: /ɪ iː/; /e eɪ/; /ɒ əʊ/;
Version 3: /r //l/

MINIMUM LEVEL

Pre-intermediate

ACTIVITY

A minimal pair discrimination game

WORKSHEETS

PronPack Worksheet 3.2
Download and print one copy for each student

AUDIO FILES

No audio with this activity

Background

A minimal pair is a pair of words or phrases with identical pronunciation except for one phoneme. For example, the words *rope* and *robe* are identical except for the final consonant sound, which is /p/ for **rope** and /b/ for **robe**. If such a sound difference does not exist in the the student's first language, they are likely to find it problematic both for understanding and in being understood. Note that the vowel sound before the unvoiced consonants /p/, /t/ and /k/ is slightly shorter than before the voiced consonants /b/, /d/ and /g/. For example, the vowel in rope sounds slightly shorter than the vowel in robe. This helps to distinguish them.

There are thee versions of *Hear Say Dominoes*:

Version 1: final unvoiced and voiced stop consonant pairs /p/ and /b/; /t/ and /d/; /k/ and /g/

Version 2: short and long vowel sound pairs /ɪ/ and /iː/; /e/ and /eɪ/; /ɒ/ and /əʊ/

Version 3: the consonant pair /r/ and /l/

Presentation

1. Draw the **DIAGRAM 3.2A** and **3.2B** on the board.

2. Explain that you will read words from the rectangles in **3.2A** and students must find the same word in a rectangle in **3.2B**. They must then say the other word in the same rectangle. For example, if you say *wrote*, students must say *coat*.

3. Point out that in this game, they must hear and pronounce the difference between /t/ and /d/ very clearly in order not to make a mistake.

4. Practise doing this a few times, with you as **A** and the class as **B**. The conversation should go as follows:

   You: *Wrote!*
   Students: *Coat!*
   You: *Road!*
   Students: *Code!*

5. Ask students to do the same in pairs, one as **A** and the other as **B**.

Activity

1. Put the students into pairs and make one member of each pair **A** and the other **B**.

2. Give out the *Worksheet 3.2* and ask them to fold it along the vertical dotted line. **Student A** should look at **Side A** and **Student B** should look at **Side B**.

3. **Student A** begins by finding the word *START* on the first domino, and saying the word at the right hand end of the same domino.

4. **Student B** must find the word they hear at the left hand end of one of their dominoes and then say the word at the right hand end of the same domino.

5. **Student A** must find the word they hear at the left hand end of one of their dominoes and then say the word at the right hand end of the same domino, and so on.

6. Students continue doing this until they reach the domino with the word *END* on it. If they have played the game correctly, they should have used all the dominoes. If they don't, or if they fail to reach *END*, they have made a mistake and should start again.

7. If appropriate, get students to change partners and play again.

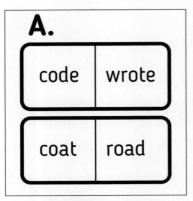

DIAGRAM 3.2A

Key

Version 1: *rode – robe – cab – coat – block – bears – log – code – wrote – wide – hard – pears – lock – rope – cap – white – heart – goat – blog*

Version 2: *bins – cost – want – feel – sells – clock – sleep – pen – sails – cloak – pepper – pain – won't – fill – beans – coast – slip – fit – paper*

Version 3: *correct – played – crowd – glow – grass – light – reader – long – fright – prayed – leader – grow – flight – right – collect – wrong – cloud – road – glass*

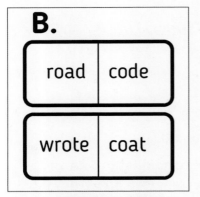

DIAGRAM 3.2B

Follow up

Tell students to unfold their worksheets and use the ten sentences at the bottom of the page to practise the same minimal pairs from the game in the context of sentences. **Student A** says a sentence containing one of the two words in brackets. **Student B** listens and says *left* or *right*.

3.2 Goes well with ...

... **Version 2** goes well with **PronPack 3.1** Version 1 and **PronPack 4.1** for a lesson on long versus short vowels.

... **Version 3** goes well with **PronPack 3.5** Version 3 and **PronPack 4.8** for a lesson on *r* versus *l*.

A

Fold along dotted line

B

1. Tie the (rope/robe) around your waist.
2. There are (pears/bears) in those woods!
3. Take a (cap/cab) if it's raining.
4. A smartphone with a (white/wide) screen?
5. He had (heart/hard) problems.
6. Who (wrote/rode) 'Black Beauty'?
7. He took his (coat/goat) up the mountain.
8. There's a (block/blog) on the Internet.
9. Put a (lock/log) on the fireplace.
10. You need to change your (coat/code).

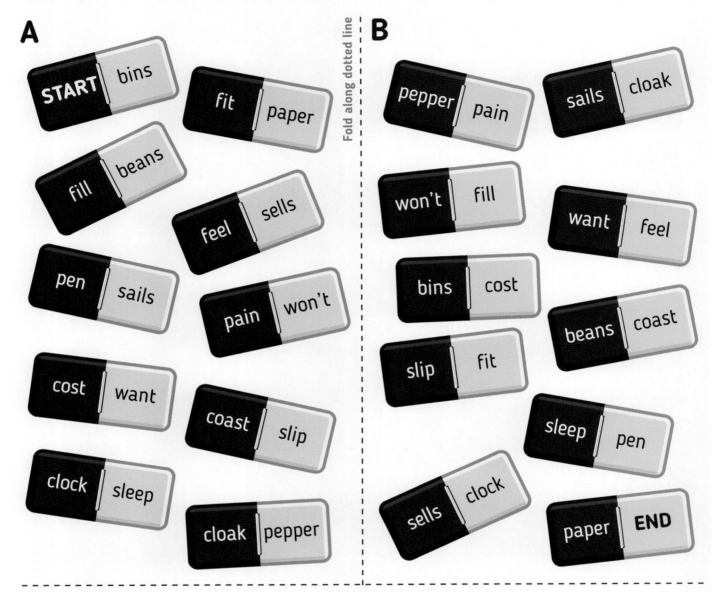

A

START | bins

fit | paper

fill | beans

feel | sells

pen | sails

pain | won't

cost | want

coast | slip

clock | sleep

cloak | pepper

B

pepper | pain

sails | cloak

won't | fill

want | feel

bins | cost

beans | coast

slip | fit

sleep | pen

sells | clock

paper | END

Fold along dotted line

1. I can see (you're fit/your feet).
2. Can you (fill/feel) it?
3. We left the (bins/beans) out.
4. Don't (slip/sleep) on the ice.
5. There's a (pen/pain) in my hand.
6. My dad (sells/sails) boats.
7. Have you got any black (pepper/paper)?
8. The (cost's/coast's) clear.
9. They (want/won't) sleep.
10. The palace has a special (clock/cloak) room.

3.2 Hear Say Dominoes – Version 3

A

Fold along dotted line

B

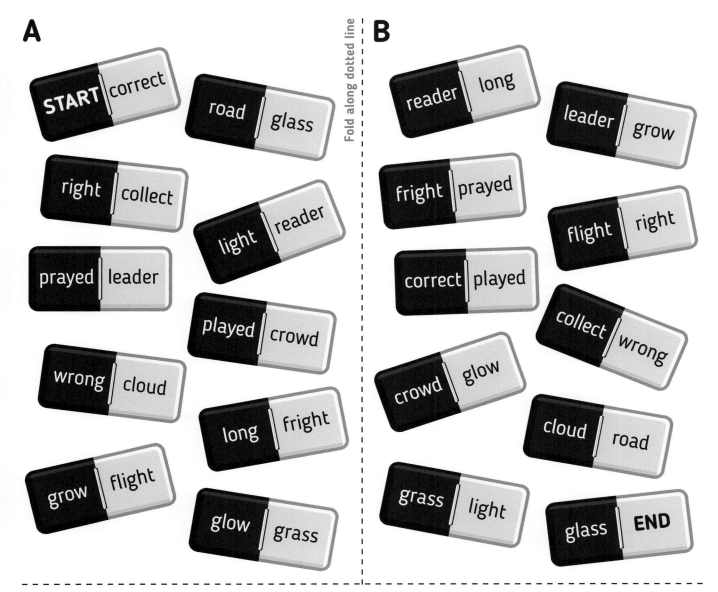

START | correct

road | glass

right | collect

light | reader

prayed | leader

played | crowd

wrong | cloud

long | fright

grow | flight

glow | grass

reader | long

leader | grow

fright | prayed

flight | right

correct | played

collect | wrong

crowd | glow

cloud | road

grass | light

glass | END

1. First turn on the (right/light), please.
2. We (prayed/played) for more goals.
3. We took the (wrong/long) way home.
4. Plants don't (grow/glow) in the dark.
5. Will you (correct/collect) my homework?

6. You must respect your (readers/leaders).
7. We were lost in the (crowds/clouds).
8. I had a terrible (fright/flight).
9. The (grass/glass) needs cutting.
10. That's a big (road/load)!

West or East

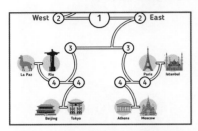

Background

A minimal pair is two words or phrases with identical pronunciation except for one phoneme. For example, the words *backs* and *packs* are identical except for the initial consonant sound, /p/ for **packs** which is and /b/ for **backs**. If such a sound difference does not exist in the student's first language, they are likely to find it problematic both for understanding and in being understood.

This game can be played with any set of minimal pairs but a sample set, contextualized in sentences, is provided in **DIAGRAM 3.3-A**.

Consonants – / p/ and /b/; /b/ and /v/; /f/ and /v/; /s/ and /z/; /r/ and /l/; /t/ and /d/;

Vowels – /ɪ/ and /iː/; /e/ and /eɪ/; /ɒ/ and /əʊ/; /æ/ and /e/; /ɔː/ and /əʊ/; /æ/ and /ʌ/.

Presentation

1. Give out *Worksheet 3.3* and explain that the starting position is the number **1** in the centre of the page. Explain that you are going to give instructions for them to reach one of the 16 destination cities at the top or bottom of the page.

2. Demonstrate how to follow the route on a worksheet, with your finger. Say *West!* Your finger goes to the **2** on the left. Say *East!*. Your finger continues up the line to the junction and then to the **3** on the right. Say *East!*. Your finger goes up the line to the junction and then to the **4** on the right. Say *West!*. Your finger goes down the line and then to the destination on the left – **Mumbai**.

3. Try your students with a few more example routes to make sure they get the idea.

4. Explain that you will do the same again, but using the words *living* and *leaving* (or any other minimal pair). Write on the board:

   living = west; leaving = East

   Give directions, for example:

   You: **1** – *leaving*; **2** – *leaving*; **3** – *living*; **4** – *living*

   Students: *Athens!*

DIAGRAM 3.3-A: MINIMAL PAIRS BANK

Consonant Pairs	Vowel Pairs
/p/ /b/ 1. They lay on their **packs/backs**. 2. He tied a **rope/robe** around his waist. 3. There's a **pear/bear** in that tree. 4. Please send me the **pills/bills**.	**/ɪ/ /iː/** 1. I'm **living/leaving** with mum. 2. Don't **hit/heat** the plates. 3. Don't **slip/sleep** on the ice. 4. Can you **fill/feel** it?
/b/ /v/ 1. I'll only wear the **best/vest**! 2. Do you want a **bet/vet**? 3. Would you like a **copy/coffee**? 4. You were driving **past/fast**.	**/e/ /eɪ/** 1. We **rest/raced** in our cars. 2. Have you **tested/tasted** the wine? 3. My dad **sells/sails** boats. 4. There's a **pen/pain** in my hand.
/f/ /v/ 1. This is where we **lift/lived**. 2. That's quite a **few/view**! 3. Ask your **wife's/wives'** friends. 4. She had a love **affair/of air**.	**/ɒ/ /əʊ/** 1. We got a **cot/coat** for the baby. 2. They would have **none/known** of it. 3. They **want/won't** sleep. 4. What a great **honour/owner**!
/s/ /z/ 1. I found ten **pence/pens** in my bag. 2. Which **piece/peas** would you like? 3. What's wrong with your **niece/knees**? 4. Which **place/plays** have you seen?	**/æ/ /e/** 1. Where did the **man/men** go? 2. This **pan's/pen's** leaking! 3. It's **sad/said** that she died young. 4. We're on the wrong **track/trek**?
/r/ /l/ 1. First turn on the **right/light**, please. 2. We took the **wrong/long** way home. 3. We were lost in the **crowds/clouds**. 4. Will you **correct/collect** my homework?	**/ɔː/ /əʊ/** 1. I **walk/woke** early in the morning. 2. Anybody **called/cold** this morning? 3. There's a mouse in the **hall/hole**! 4. She's **pausing/posing** for a photo.
/t/ /d/ 1. A university **town/down** in the south. 2. I've forgotten my **coat/code**! 3. Wear your jacket and **tie/die**! 4. He had **heart/hard** problems.	**/æ/ /ʌ/** 1. There's a **cat/cut** on the sofa! 2. I **ran/run** for half an hour. 3. I collected coins in my **cup/cap**. 4. I didn't enjoy that **match/much**.

Note that each of the sentences above contains a minimal pair written in bold e.g. **packs/backs** with the option to choose either of the words to direct the students *West* or *East*.

If you say the first word of the pair, to the left of the slash e.g. **packs/**, students should go *West*, if you say the second of the two words in bold on the right of the slash e.g. **/backs**, they should go *East*.

Activity

1. Give out a set of minimal pairs in sentences on a slip of paper, or write them on the board. Demonstrate the game by giving directions to one of the cities using the minimal pairs in sentences. You can use one of the sets in the *Minimal Pairs Bank* **DIAGRAM 3.3-A**.

   The example below uses the Vowel Pairs /ɪ/ /iː/. If you say the first word of the minimal pair written in bold, students should go *West*, if you say the second, they should go *East*:

   You: 1 – *I'm leaving with mum;* **2** – *Don't heat the plates;* **3** – *Don't sleep on the ice;* **4** – *Can you fill it?*

   Students: *Paris!*

2. Repeat this step several times. If students get to the wrong city, ask them to work out where things went wrong. Explain that **both** you, the speaker, and they, the listeners, are responsible for the error.

   If the speaker doesn't get the message across to the listener the first time, both should try again, exaggerating the difference to make sure the listener chooses the intended word.

3. Get students to do the same in pairs or small groups, with one speaking and the other(s) listening and following the route. They can repeat this as many times as necessary.

Flexi: In order to do this game, students do not need to produce exact vowel qualities – they merely need to distinguish pairs of sounds consistently.

3.3 Goes well with ...

... **Vowel pairs** – **PronPack 1.6**, **PronPack 2.3**, **PronPack 3.1** Version 2 and **PronPack 4.2** for a lesson on short vowels.

... **Consonant pairs** – **PronPack 1.7**, **PronPack 3.4** Version 1 and **PronPack 4.11** for a lesson on stop consonants.

... **Consonant pairs** – **PronPack 1.8**, **PronPack 2.2** Version 2, **PronPack 3.4** Version 3, **PronPack 4.9** and **4.10** for a lesson on fricatives and affricates.

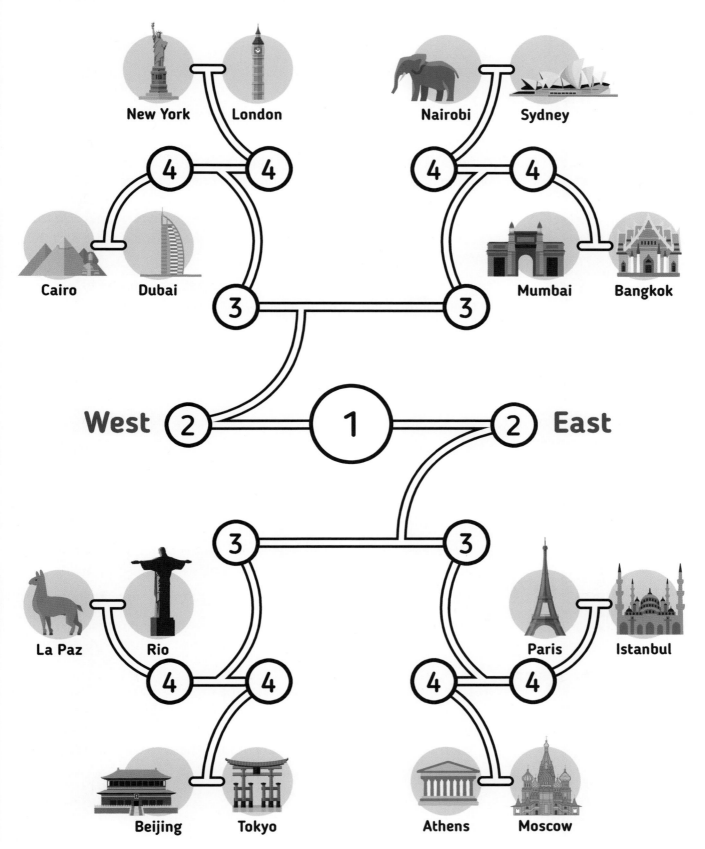

Street Maps

3.4

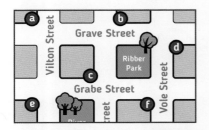

Background

A minimal pair is a pair of words or phrases with identical pronunciation except for one phoneme. For example, *dock* and *dog* are identical except for the final consonant sound, which is /k/ for **dock** and /g/ for **dog**. If such a sound difference does not exist in the student's first language, they are likely to find it problematic both for understanding and in being understood.

On each version there are four different street map games, offering practice in the following consonant sound minimal pairs:

Version 1: /b/ and /v/; /p/ and /b/; /k/ and /g/; /m/ and /n/

Version 2: /t/ and /d/; /s/ and /θ/; /v/ and /w/; /z/ and /ð/

Version 3: /s/ and /ʃ/; /tʃ/ and /ʃ/; /j/ and /dʒ/; /tʃ/ and /dʒ/

Presentation

1. Give out a single page from *Worksheet 3.3* with four street maps, or just one of the street maps trimmed from it.

2. Write the following sentence frame on the board:

   It's on the corner of _____ and _____ (opposite _____ Park).

   Complete it using names from a map on the sheet, for example on **Street Maps Version 1** (the /b/ /v/ map), write:

   *It's on the corner of **Grabe Street** and **Bole Street** (opposite **River Park**).*

3. Explain that the places marked *a – i* on the map are cafés. Ask students to identify which café the sentence on the board describes – in this case, **C**.

4. Give spoken directions to some of the other cafés on the map, using the same sentence structure. The part in brackets is optional, depending on whether there is a park opposite or not. If students want to request clarification, encourage them to use this form:

   Sorry, did you say Grave Street?

Activity

1. Put the students into pairs or small groups. Tell one of the students to give directions to a cafe, using the sentence structure from the board. The others listen and identify the cafe. Students take turns to give directions.

2. If you are using a page with more than one map, students can repeat the activity a number of times with each map, and then decide which one presented the most pronunciation difficulties.

Flexi: Many speakers of English do not pronounce the sounds /θ/ and /ð/ (found in **Version 2**), replacing them with /t/ and /d/ or /f/ and /v/ respectively.

3.4 Goes well with ...

... **Version 1** goes well with **PronPack 1.7**, **PronPack 3.3** consonant pairs and **PronPack 4.11** for a lesson on stop consonants.

... **Version 2** goes well with **PronPack 2.2** Version 2 and **PronPack 4.7** for a lesson on semi-vowels.

... **Version 3** goes well with **PronPack 1.8**, **PronPack 2.2** Version 2, **PronPack 3.3** consonant pairs, **PronPack 4.9** and **4.10** for a lesson on fricatives and affricates.

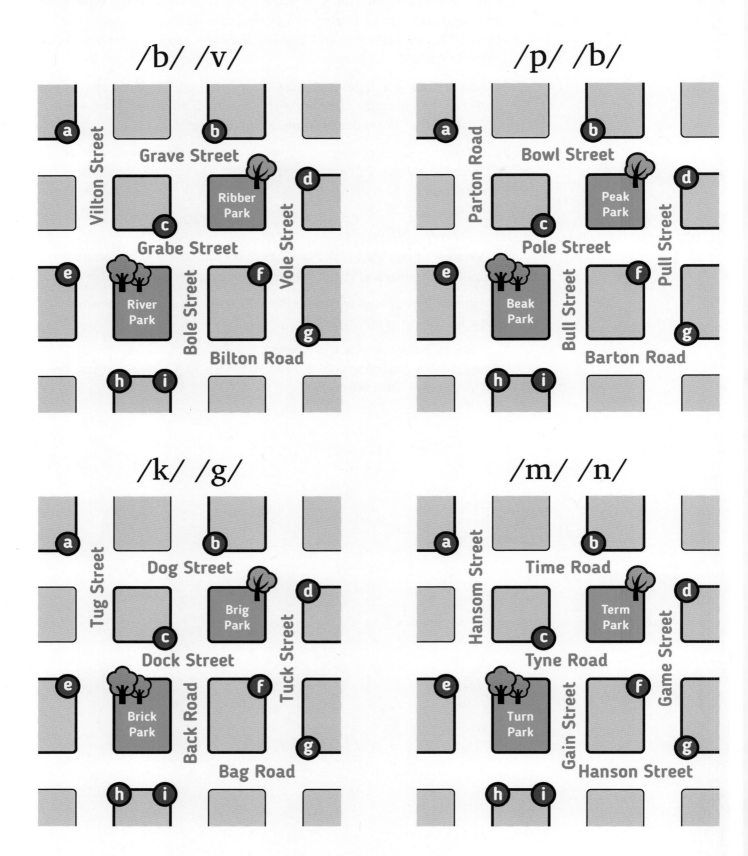

3.4 Street Maps – Version 2

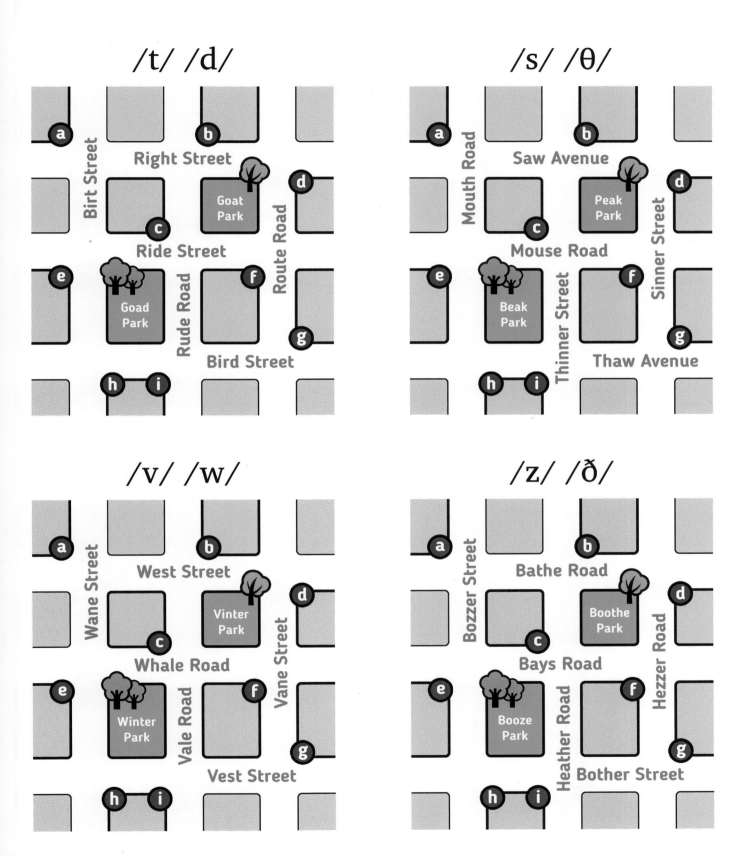

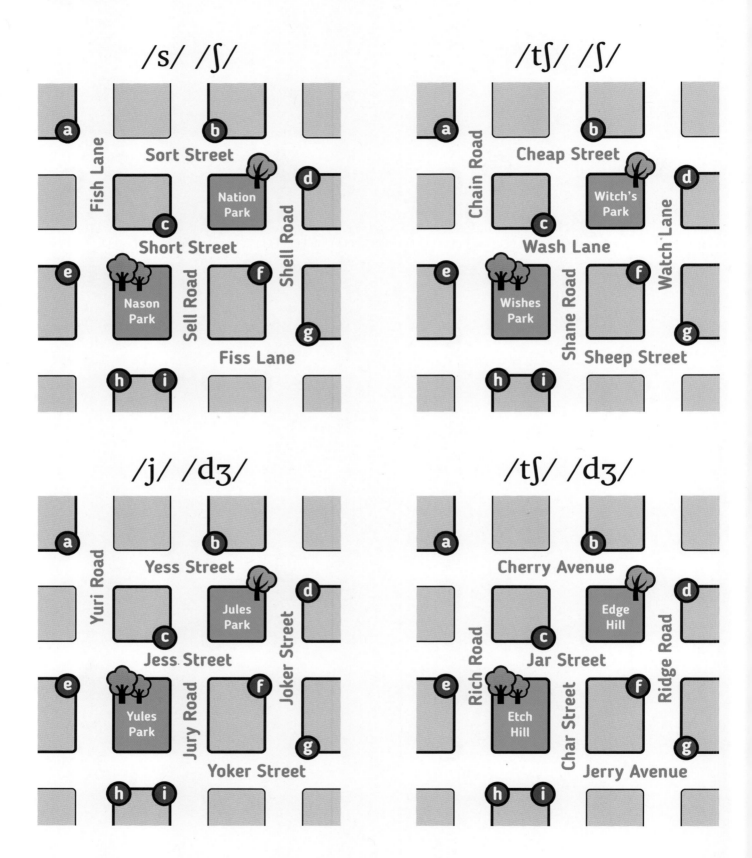

Box Sets

3.5

TEACHING FOCUS

To practise perceiving and producing the difference between minimal pairs:
Version 1: /ɪ iː/; /eə ɪə/; /e eɪ/;
Version 2: /s z/; /ʃ tʃ/; /t d/;
Version 3: /l r/

MINIMUM LEVEL

Pre-intermediate

ACTIVITY

A minimal pair discrimination game

WORKSHEETS

PronPack Worksheet 3.5
Download and print one copy for each student

AUDIO FILES

No audio with this activity

Background

A minimal pair is a pair of words or phrases with identical pronunciation except for one phoneme. For example, *sit* and *seat* are identical except for the vowel sound, which is /ɪ/ for **sit** and /iː/ for **seat**. There are three versions of Box Sets:

Version 1: Vowel pairs /ɪ/ and /iː/; /eə / and /ɪə/; /e / and /eɪ/

Version 2: Consonant pairs /s/ and /z/; /ʃ/ and /tʃ/; /t / and /d/

Version 3: Minimal pair /l/ and /r/

Presentation

1. Give out one page from *Worksheet 3.5* and ask students to look at the first set. Say a phrase and ask students to identify which **picture A-D** you are referring to. For instance, on **Version 1**, **Set 1**:

    You: *Sit on a sheep?*
    Students : *Picture C*
    You: *Seat on a ship?*
    Students : *Picture B*

Activity

1. Get the students into pairs or small groups. Tell one student to say the phrase for one of the pictures. The others listen and identify the picture. Students take turns to be the speaker.

2. Students repeat the activity a number of times, and then move on to the next box set.

3. Finally, ask students to say which box set on the page caused most pronunciation difficulties.

3.5 Goes well with ...

... **Version 2** goes well with **PronPack 2.2** Version 2 and **PronPack 4.15** for a lesson on *s* versus *z* and *–s* endings.

... **Version 3** goes well with **PronPack 3.2** Version 3 and **PronPack 4.8** for a lesson on *r* versus *l*.

1. /ɪ/ /iː/

A sit on a ship	**B** seat on a ship
C sit on a sheep	**D** seat on a sheep

A the bear's here	**B** the bear's hair
C the beer's here	**D** the beer's hair

2. /eə/ /ɪə/

3. /e/ /eɪ/

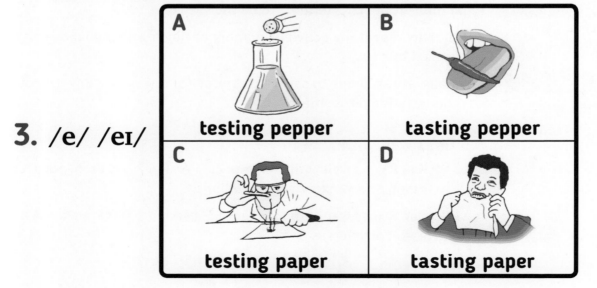

A testing pepper	**B** tasting pepper
C testing paper	**D** tasting paper

A the prize of peace	**B** the prize of peas
C the price of peas	**D** the price of peace

1. /s/ /z/

2. /ʃ/ /tʃ/

A washing ships	**B** watching ships
C washing chips	**D** watching chips

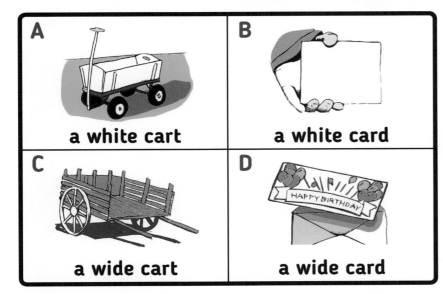

A a white cart	**B** a white card
C a wide cart	**D** a wide card

3. /t/ /d/

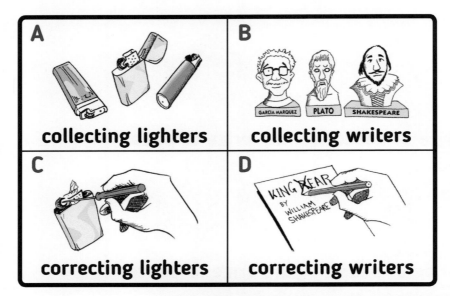

1. /l/ /r/

A collecting lighters
B collecting writers
C correcting lighters
D correcting writers

2. /l/ /r/

A the pilot's alive
B the pirates arrive
C the pilots arrive
D the pirate's alive

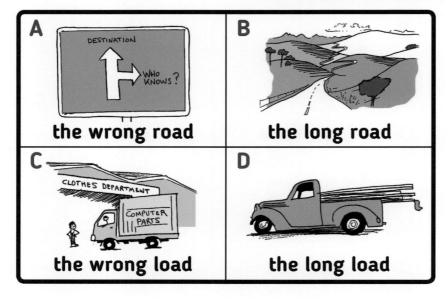

A the wrong road
B the long road
C the wrong load
D the long load

3. /l/ /r/

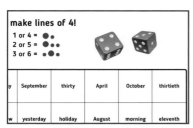

	September	thirty	April	October	thirtieth
w	yesterday	holiday	August	morning	eleventh

TEACHING FOCUS

To raise awareness of stress in some common words and phrases relating to time and number.

MINIMUM LEVEL

Elementary

ACTIVITY

A dice and grid game. **Please note** One dice is needed for each pair or group of students

WORKSHEETS

PronPack Worksheet 3.6 Download and print one copy for each student

AUDIO FILES

No audio with this activity

Background

In words and phrases in English which have more than one syllable, one of the syllables will have more stress than the others. For example, the word *Saturday* has three syllables, and the first one has is stressed. Consequently, **Saturday** has the stress pattern **Ooo**.

In this game, students will match words and phrases relating to time and number with the stress patterns **Oo** (eg *April*), **Ooo** (eg *Saturday*) and **oOo** (eg *eleventh*).

Presentation

1. Write the words below on the board and drill the pronunciation. Ask students to say how many syllables each word contains.

   Saturday   April   eleventh

2. Write the stress patterns below on the board.

   Oo Ooo   oOo

3. Ask students to match the patterns with words in the phrase. Point out that the big circle represents the syllable which is said more strongly in the word. It stands out from the others by being higher, louder or longer than the other syllables – or all of these.

4. Explain that the class will play a game using dice. Each number on the dice will correspond to one of the three stress patterns.

Activity

1. Divide class into pairs. Give each pair a dice and *Worksheet 3.6*. Explain that in this game, the objective is for players to win lines of four squares. These may be horizontal, vertical or diagonal.

2. Players take turns to throw the dice. Each number corresponds to one of the stress patterns shown at the top of the page. The player can then win one of any of the squares in the grid containing a word or phrase with this pattern. For example, if a player throws 2, they can win the square containing **Saturday**.

3. When a player wins a square, they can write the first letter of their name, or another symbol, in that square.

4. When a player has won a line of 4 squares, they may draw a line through those four squares, horizontally, vertically or diagonally, see **DIAGRAM 3.6A**.

5. The game continues until all the squares are used. If there are no more words left with one of the stress patterns, the player misses a turn.

6. When all the squares are used, players count the number of lines of they have won. The player with the most lines is the winner.

3.6 Goes well with ...

... **PronPack 2.9** for a lesson introducing word stress.

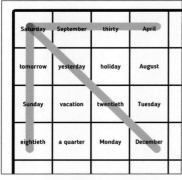

DIAGRAM 3.6A

Try to make lines of 4!

1 or 4 = ●●
2 or 5 = ●●●
3 or 6 = ●●●

Saturday	September	thirty	April	October	thirtieth
tomorrow	yesterday	holiday	August	morning	eleventh
Sunday	vacation	twentieth	Tuesday	seventy	November
eightieth	a quarter	Monday	December	century	Thursday
a hundred	fiftieth	Friday	a thousand	dinner time	sixtieth
ninetieth	eleven	seven	mid-morning	twenty	midnight

Pronunciation Pairworks

3.7 One Stress or Two?

TEACHING FOCUS

To practise perceiving and producing stress in compound nouns.

MINIMUM LEVEL

Intermediate

ACTIVITY

A stress minimal pair discrimination game

WORKSHEETS

PronPack Worksheet 3.7
Download and print one copy for each student

AUDIO FILES

No audio with this activity

Background

A stress minimal pair is a pair of words or phrases which are the same except for the stress pattern. For example, the compound noun *wetsuit* and the adjective + noun *wet suit* have different stress patterns: *wetsuit* = **Oo**; *wet suit* = **OO**.

This reflects the following rule: all content words have one stressed syllable. Since *wetsuit* is only one word, it has only one stressed syllable. Since *wet* and *suit* are two words, there are two stressed syllables. But note that sometimes, a compound noun may appear to be two words. For example, *bus stop* appears to be two words, but it is one compound noun, and has the pattern **Oo**.

Presentation

1. Give out *Worksheet 3.7*. Tell students to look at the example sentence and say it, first with the compound noun **a**, and then with the noun + verb combination **b**. Make sure you stress the words in **bold**.

   a *I need to change out of this* **wet***suit*

   b *I need to change out of this* **wet suit**

2. Say one of the sentences again and ask students to identify if you are saying **a** or **b**.

3. Follow the same procedure with items **1-6**.

Activity

1. Put students into pairs or small groups. Tell one student to say the sentence with **a** or **b** for each item. The others listen and identify the picture **a** or **b**. Students take turns to be the speaker.

2. Students repeat the activity a number of times and then move on to the next item.

wetsuit = 1 stress (● •)
wet suit = 2 stresses (● ●)

Example: I need to change out of this ......   a. **wet**suit   b. **wet suit**

1. I didn't see the ...

a. **bus** stop

b. **bus stop**

2. We didn't visit the ...

a. **White** House

b. **white house**

3. This is a picture of a ...

a. **black**bird

b. **black bird**

4. Did you see ...?

a. the **butch**er's shop

b. the **butch**ers **shop**

5. My sister went out with a ...

a. **long** jumper

b. **long jumper**

6. Would you mind cleaning the ...?

a. **black**board

b. **black board**

Stress Pinball

3.8

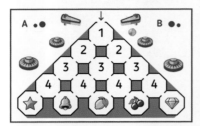

TEACHING FOCUS

To learn typical stress patterns of 2-syllable verbs and nouns; to raise awareness of how vowel sounds change in stressed and unstressed syllables.

MINIMUM LEVEL

Intermediate

ACTIVITY

A stress minimal pair discrimination game

WORKSHEETS

PronPack Worksheet 3.8 Download and print one copy for each student, or pair of students

AUDIO FILES

Background

A stress minimal pair is a pair of word which appear the same but have a different stress pattern. For example, the verb *protest* has the pattern **oO**, while the noun *protest* has the pattern **Oo**. The vowel sounds may also differ in such word pairs, for example the first vowel in the verb *protest* is /ə/ while in the noun it is /əʊ/. Such differences are a consequence of the difference in stress: vowels are often reduced to /ə/ in unstressed syllables.

There is a general pattern that English 2-syllable verbs have stress on the 2nd syllable (60%) and 2-syllable nouns have stress on the 1st (90%). This lesson highlights this by focusing on a small set of words which are both verbs and nouns, but with differing stress accordingly, such as *protest*.

Presentation

1. Give out *Worksheet 3.8*. Read **Sentence 1A** and check students understand the meaning of the verb *protest* (to show you disagree with something by carrying signs, shouting or standing somewhere).

   Read **Phrase 1B** and point out that the word *protest* is a noun. Elicit or explain that the phrase refers to the action of a particular group of workers.

2. Model the verb and noun pronunciation of *protest*, highlighting the difference in stress and first vowel sound (in the verb, it is a short sound, in the noun it is long). Do a minimal pair activity, randomly saying the verb or noun form for the class to say **A** or **B**.

3. Repeat with **2A** and **B**. Elicit or explain the meaning of **Sentence A** (*rebel* **oO** = many families are fighting against something) and **Phrase B** (*rebel* **Oo** = a person in a family, who is fighting against something).

   Highlight the difference in stress and vowel sounds in the first and second syllables. Do a minimal pair activity, randomly saying the verb or noun form for the class to say **A** or **B**.

4. Tell students that these are the most common stress patterns for 2-syllable verbs and nouns in English (although there are many exceptions, of course)

5. Read all the pairs of sentences (or use *Audio 3.8-1*) and ask students to repeat.

Note: The words **object** and **refuse** have a completely different meaning as verbs and nouns:
object oO *(verb)* = to express opposition to something (equivalent noun = objection), **object** Oo *(noun)* = a physical thing you can touch (but not living)
refuse oO *(verb)* = to say you do not accept something (equivalent noun = refusal) **refuse** Oo *(noun)* = rubbish; garbage

MORE IDEAS
Ask students to find sentences containing the verb-noun words in this game. They can do this online in a search engine, or in the example sentences in a dictionary. They then try to say the sentence with the correct pronunciation.

Activity

1. Demonstrate how the *Pinball* diagram works. Tell your students to place their fingers on the number one. Explain that if you say **A**, they must move downward to the left, and if you say **B**, they must move downward to the right.

2. Say: **1 – A; 2 – A; 3 – B; 4 – A**. Ask the students which shape they have reached (*answer = bell*). Repeat this with other sequences to reach the other shapes (star, lemon, cherries or diamond) until you are sure they have understood the idea of the game.

3. Demonstrate the game. Tell students you will say phrases **1-4**, randomly choosing either **Version A** or **Version B**. Explain that they should follow the path on the *Pinball* diagram just as they did in **Step 2**.

4. Say your four phrases (or play *Audio 3.8-2*) and check that the students have all reached the intended shape. Repeat this step a few times (there are three different routes on the audio).

5. Tell students to practise in pairs or small groups, taking turns to speak and listen. One student says the sentences and the listeners follow the route on the *Pinball* diagram. The objective is for all of the listeners to reach the shape the speaker intended. If they fail, the speaker must try again and exaggerate the difference more.

Note: If you find that students are having difficulty reaching the intended shape, you may need to return to focusing on the pronunciation of the verb-noun pairs.

Drill them and tell students to exaggerate the strength of the stressed syllable and the shortness of the unstressed syllable.

3.8 Goes well with ...

... **PronPack 1.10**, **PronPack 2.7** and **PronPack 4.16** for a lesson on word stress families.

A •●   B ●•

A •●	B ●•
1. The workers pro<u>test</u> /prəˈtest/	The worker's <u>pro</u>test /ˈprəʊtest/
2. The families re<u>bel</u> /rɪˈbel/	The family's <u>re</u>bel /ˈrebəl/
3. Their stories con<u>flict</u> /kənˈflɪkt/	Their story's <u>con</u>flict /ˈkɒnflɪkt/
4. The countries ex<u>port</u> /ɪkˈspɔː⁽ʳ⁾t/	The country's <u>ex</u>port /ˈekspɔː⁽ʳ⁾t/
5. The flavours con<u>trast</u> /kənˈtrɑːst/	The flavour's <u>con</u>trast /ˈkɒntrɑːst/
6. The students pre<u>sent</u> /prɪˈzent/	The student's <u>pre</u>sent /ˈprezənt/
7. The singers re<u>cord</u> /rɪˈkɔː⁽ʳ⁾d/	The singer's <u>re</u>cord /ˈrekɔː⁽ʳ⁾d/
8. The owners ob<u>ject</u> /əbˈdʒekt/	The owner's <u>ob</u>ject /ˈɒbdʒekt/
9. Their profits in<u>crease</u> /ɪŋˈkriːs/	Their profit's <u>in</u>crease /ˈɪŋkriːs/
10. Their clients up<u>grade</u> /ʌpˈgreɪd/	Their client's <u>up</u>grade /ˈʌpgreɪd/
11. The soldiers de<u>sert</u> /dɪˈzɜː⁽ʳ⁾t/	The soldier's <u>de</u>sert /ˈdezə⁽ʳ⁾t/
12. The neighbours re<u>fuse</u> /rɪˈfjuːz/	The neighbour's <u>re</u>fuse /ˈrefjuːs/

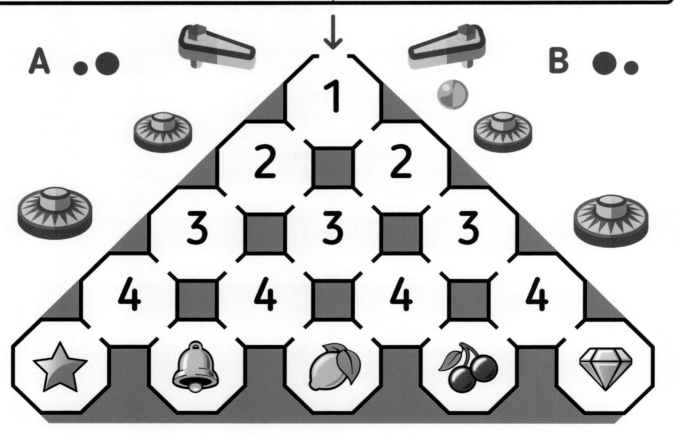

Sound Bites

3.9

I scream

Ice cream

TEACHING FOCUS

To raise awareness of word and phrasal homophones.

MINIMUM LEVEL

Pre-intermediate

ACTIVITY

A listen-and-find game

WORKSHEETS

PronPack Worksheet 3.9
Download and print copies of **Worksheet A** for half the class and **Worksheet B** for the other half.

AUDIO FILES

Background

In English, there are many pairs of words which have a different meaning and spelling but are pronounced the same, such as **way** and **weigh** (both pronounced /weɪ/). These are known as homophones. Groups of words – here, we call them 'sound bites' - may also be homophones, such as **I scream** and **ice cream**. In this case, the two sound bites are identical because the words are joined and we cannot hear where one word finishes and the next word starts. This is normal in natural spoken English.

In this activity, all of the sound bites **1-10** on **Worksheet A** have a corresponding sound bite **a-k** on **Worksheet B**. They have a different meaning but identical pronunciation.

Presentation

1. Write the names **Dan** and **Anne** on the board. Explain that you are going to dictate a sentence involving these two characters and ask your students to write down what they hear.

2. Say the sentence, *Someone called Anne said "Someone call Dan!"*. Make sure you say it joined up with no gaps between the words. You can repeat it a few times.

3. Compare different answers around the class. You may get different variations such as, *"Someone call Dan!" Said someone called Anne*. Explain that, because the two sound bites **call Dan** and **called Anne** are identical, there were many possible ways of interpreting what you hear.

Activity

1. Divide class into pairs. Give one member of each pair **Worksheet A** and the other **Worksheet B**. Tell them to make sure their partner can't see their worksheets.

2. Direct students to the picture which is at the top of both worksheets. Say the two sound bites **I scream** and **ice cream**, making sure you say them so that they sound the same. Ask students if they can hear the difference, and elicit that they are the same.

3. Tell students to work with their partner and take turns to read out the description of one of the pictures on their worksheet. The other listens to find a similar sound bite on their own worksheet. Once they've found it, they read it aloud.

4. Once students have found a matching pair, ask them to read them out a few times to each other to see if they sound the same or different.

5. When students have matched all the pictures on their worksheets, tell them to compare sheets. They may be surprised to find how different the meanings of the matching sound bites are!

6. Explain that the matching sound bites on the two sheets are be pronounced the same. Ask students to practise saying the sound bites so that they sound identical for both sheets. If they find this impossible, you can say the sentences yourself or play *Audio 3.9-1*

Key

The matching pairs are:

1 – d, 2 – f, 3 – e, 4 – g, 5 – c, 6 – h, 7 – i, 8 – a, 9 – j, 10 – b

3.9 Goes well with ...

... **PronPack 2.5** and **2.10** for a lesson on connected speech.

Example: **I scream**

Ice cream

1   I wake early

2

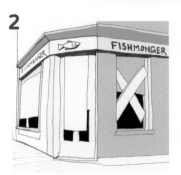

It sold fish

3

I lie quite a lot

4

I saw Kate stop

5

Great eyes

6

Find answers

7

Dan!

Someone call Dan!

8   Sick spies

9

Watch or a dress?

10   It was once wetter

Example: **I scream**

Ice cream

a **Six pies**

b

It was one sweater

c **Grey ties**

d **I weigh Curly**

e

I like white alot

f

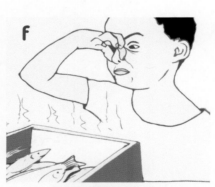

It's old fish

g

I saw Kate's top

h

Fine dancers

i

Someone called Anne

j

What's your address?

Eye Witness

3.10

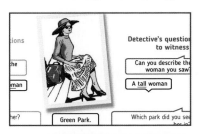

TEACHING FOCUS

To practise tonic stress placement for given and new information.

MINIMUM LEVEL

Pre-intermediate

ACTIVITY

Interview role-play with appropriate stress

WORKSHEETS

PronPack Worksheet 3.10
Download and print one copy for each student

AUDIO FILES

Background

In an English tone unit, the tonic stress is normally on the last content word. For example, in the response *A tall woman*, the word **wom**an would normally be stressed. However, if the word *woman* has already appeared in the conversation, it is not new any more. In this case, the word ***tall*** may be stressed instead. When stress depends on the context in this way, it is called ***tonic stress***.

Not all languages use tonic stress in this way – they may change the word order instead for the same effect. For this reason, it requires plenty of practice.

Presentation

1. Show the class a picture of a person in a public place. It may be a photo cut from a magazine or projected from the internet. Show the picture for a minute or two and then remove it. Now explain that this person was involved in a crime, and they are witnesses and must tell you everything they can remember about the appearance of the person.

2. Write these two phrases on the board:

   A   *A tall **wom**an*

   B   *A **tall** woman*

   Read them out, placing the stress on the bold, underlined word. Now read them several times in random order. The students must identify if you are saying **A** or **B**.

3. Give out the worksheet. Explain how it is laid out:

   Witness 1 = A detective's questions to the first witness.

   Middle column = The answers from both Witness 1 and Witness 2.

   Witness 2 = The detective's questions to the second witness.

4. Point out that **Witness 1** and **Witness 2** both give exactly the same answers, but with different pronunciation.

5. Point to the two phrases on the board and ask students to match the phrases with **Witness 1** or **2** on the worksheet.

6. Elicit that, in **2**, _**tall**_ is stressed because this is new information – the word _woman_ is already there in the question. This is not the case in **1** – the question doesn't specify if the person is a man or a woman.

7. (Optional) Play _Audio 3.10-1_ for the students to hear the two conversations. Ask them to pay attention to the word the witnesses stress.

MORE IDEAS

Students invent their own witness interviews similar to the ones in the activity, but with different specific details.

Activity

1. Ask students to work in groups of three. One is a police officer, the other two are the witnesses. Explain that they are going to role-play the two conversations. Before they begin, ask each 'witness' to decide which word they will need to stress in their answer.

   If you can't make groups of three, students could do the activity in pairs, with the same person role-playing the 1st and the 2nd witness.

2. Get some of the groups/pairs to perform their role-plays to the class. The class listen to check the witnesses stress the appropriate word.

3. Read out the answers in random order and ask the class to say if they are from **Witness 1** or **2**, for example:

   You: _**Green**_ _Park._
   Students: _Witness 2_

4. Ask students to do the same in pairs.

3.10 Goes well with ...

... **PronPack 1.13**, **PronPack 2.9**, **PronPack 3.11** and **3.12** for a lesson on tonic stress.

Detective's questions to witness 1

Can you describe the person you saw?

A tall <u>woman</u>

Where did you see her?

Did you notice what she was wearing?

And what else was she wearing?

Was she wearing anything on her face?

Did she have anything on her head?

What was she wearing on her feet?

And was she carrying anything?

Thank you. That's all

Detective's questions to witness 2

Can you describe the woman you saw?

A <u>tall</u> woman

Which park did you see her in?

What colour sweater did she have on?

And what colour skirt was she wearing?

What kind of glasses did she have?

And how would you describe her hat?

Did you notice the colour of her shoes?

What kind of bag did she have?

Thank you. That's all.

Replies from witness 1 and witness 2

Green Park.

A pale sweater.

A white skirt.

Dark glasses.

A big hat.

Black shoes.

A leather bag.

Pronunciation Pairworks 3.11 Response Questions

e Beatles.	Who do **you** like?	
eatles.	Who **do** you like?	
pecially.	**Who** do you like?	

the beach.	Where **have** you been?	To Scotland!
ere nice.		
home.	Where have you **been**?	
o London.		

Background

In an English tone unit, the tonic stress is normally on the last content word. For example, in the question *Where have you been?*, the word *been* would normally be stressed in a conversation. However, a speaker can choose to stress any of the words in the question. For instance, they can stress *you* to contrast with *I*, or *have* to contrast with *haven't*, or *Where* to contrast with *When*.

Not all languages use tonic stress in this way – they may change the word order instead for the same effect. For this reason, it requires plenty of practice.

Presentation

1. Give out the worksheet and ask students to read the exchanges in **Grid 1**. Read out the exchanges with a volunteer student, for example, **Exchange A** would be:

   Student: *I hate the Beatles.*
   You: *Who do you **like**?*
   Student: *One Direction!*

2. Point out that the pronunciation of the response question in the middle column is different in the four exchanges **A-D** because a different word is stressed in each. Elicit why.

   Suggested answers:

   A: *Like* is stressed to contrast with **hate**.

   B: *You* is stressed to contrast with **my mum**.

   C: *Do* is stressed to contrast with **don't**.

   D: *Who* is stressed to ask for more information about the vague reference **one band**.

3. Drill the pronunciation of the four response questions. Say the response questions in random order and ask students to say **A**, **B**, **C** or **D**. Then ask students to do the same as a class or in pairs.

Activity

1. Put students in pairs and ask them to fill in the missing response questions in **2-4**. The actual words are provided in the example given – they just need to write it with the appropriate word written bigger and underlined to show the stress.

2. Check the **_answers_** as a class (or let them listen to *Audio 3.11-1* to check).

   2B. _Where_ have you been?
   2D. Where have **_you_** been?

   3A. When did **_you_** get up?
   3B. When **_did_** you get up?
   3C. _When_ did you get up?

   4A. What do you **_do_**?
   4B. What **_do_** you do?
   4C. What do **_you_** do?

3. Ask the pairs of students to rehearse the mini-dialogues. Allow them to change the answer to make it relevant to themselves, for example, they could say another band instead of *One Direction*.

4. Ask pairs of students to perform their dialogues for the rest of the class in random order, but missing off the statement from the beginning. The rest of the class say which response question from **A-D** they heard.

3.11 Goes well with ...

... **PronPack 1.13, PronPack 2.9, PronPack 3.10** and **3.12** for a lesson on tonic stress.

	statement	response question	answer
1.	A. I hate The Beatles.	Who do you **like**?	One Direction!
	B. My mum likes The Beatles.	Who do **you** like?	
	C. I don't like The Beatles.	Who **do** you like?	
	D. I like one band especially.	**Who** do you like?	

	statement	response question	answer
2.	A. I haven't been to the beach.	Where **have** you been?	To Scotland!
	B. I've been somewhere nice.		
	C. I've just got back home.	Where have you **been**?	
	D. My sister's been to London.		

	statement	response question	answer
3.	A. My brother got up very late.		At ten!
	B. I didn't get up for work.		
	C. I got up really late.		
	D. I've been up for hours.	When did you **get up**?	

	statement	response question	answer
4.	A. I work for the government.		I'm a spy!
	B. I don't work in a company.		
	C. My partner's a teacher.		
	D. I do something interesting.	**What** do you do?	

Pronunciation Pairworks 3.12

Contrastive Shapes

Background

In an English question, the tonic stress is normally placed on the last content word. For example, in *Have you got a white **arrow**?*, the word arrow would normally be stressed. However, the speaker may stress another word to contrast with one which has appeared earlier in the conversation, for example, *Have you got a **black** arrow?* If stress depends on the context in this way, it is called tonic stress.

Not all languages use tonic stress in this way – they may change the word order instead for the same effect. For this reason, it requires plenty of practice.

Presentation

1. Write the short dialogue below on the board:

   A: *Where are you from?*

   B: *(Egypt). Where are **you** from?*

   A: *(Spain).*

   Elicit from the students why **you** in the second line is stressed (to contrast with the *you* in the first line). Ask students to have mini-dialogues around the class, substituting names of other countries for the ones in brackets.

2. Give out the handout. Ask students to look at the dialogue at the top of the page and answer the questions:

   - *What are Jim and Ana doing?* (playing a guessing game)

   - *What do you think the rules of the game are?* (one person chooses four shapes, the other person has to ask questions to find out which shapes the other has chosen).

   - *Why are some words underlined?* (to contrast with information in the previous question).

3. Check students know the names of the four shapes (***arrow***, ***triangle***, ***star***, ***heart***).

4. Say sentences such as the following. Ask students to repeat, making sure they exaggerate the emphasis.

*Have you got a **big** white triangle?*

*Have you got a small black **heart**?*

*Have you got a **short** black arrow?*

5. Ask volunteers around the class to make similar sentences. The rest of the class listen and say which word they heard emphasized.

6. (Optional) Play *Audio 3.12.1* of Jim and Ana playing the whole game, to answer the question - *How many questions does Jim ask?*

Activity

1. Put students in pairs. Explain that they are going to play a guessing game. The winner is the person who guesses the other player's shapes in fewer guesses.

2. Each student draws an outline around a group of **four shapes** on the handout without letting their partner see it.

3. First of all, **Player A** must guess the four shapes in **Player B**'s outline by asking questions as in *Jim* and *Ana*'s dialogue at the top of the page.

   Player B can answer only *Yes, I have* or *No, I haven't*. **B** makes a note of the number of questions which **A** asks.

4. Now, **Player B** must guesses the four shapes in **A**'s outline, following the same procedure.

5 Finally, players compare the number of questions they asked. The player who asked fewer questions is the winner.

3.12 Goes well with ...

... PronPack 1.13, PronPack 2.9, PronPack 3.10 and 3.11 for a lesson on tonic stress.

Jim: Have you got a white arrow?
Ana: No, I haven't.

Jim: Have you got a **black** arrow?
Ana: Yes, I have.

Jim: Have you got a **long** black arrow?
Ana: No, I haven't.

Jim: Right, ok. So you've got a **short** black arrow.

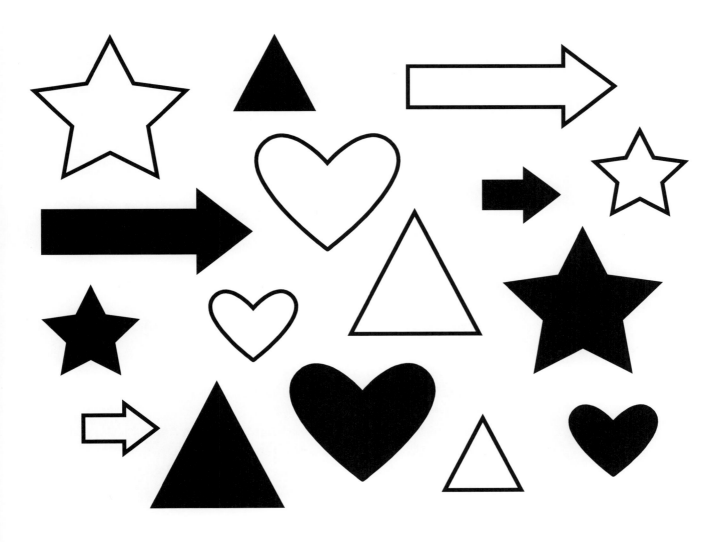

About the Author

Mark Hancock started teaching English over 30 years ago and wrote his first English language teaching book – *Pronunciation Games* – over 20 years ago. His approach in both teaching and writing ELT materials is to engage the learner and inspire their intrinsic interest in the content and in the process of the lesson. This is driven by his belief that teaching and learning a language can and should be an enjoyable experience.

He studied Geography and Philosophy at St. Andrews University, followed by teacher training courses and finally an MA in Teaching English from Aston University. Mark has taught in Sudan, Turkey, Brazil, Spain and currently lives and works in the UK. Apart from teaching and writing, he also presents at international conferences and leads on short teacher training courses.

In his free time, Mark plays the saxophone and guitar, paints in oils and walks in the mountains.

By the same author

ELT Pronunciation and Skills

- *Pronunciation Games* (CUP 1995)
- *English Pronunciation in Use Intermediate* (CUP 2003, 2012)
- *Authentic Listening Resource Pack* (Delta 2014 – co-authored with Annie McDonald)
- *Pen Pictures 1, 2 & 3* (OUP 1999 – 2000 – co-authored with Annie McDonald)
- *Oxford Advanced Learner's Dictionary 9th Ed 'Speaking Tutor' section* (OUP 2015)
- *Empower C1 'Everyday English' sections* (CUP 2016)
- *Singing Grammar* (CUP 1999)

ELT Course Book Series

- *English Result* (OUP 2007 – 2010 – co-authored with Annie McDonald)
- *Out and About* (CUP 2015 – co-authored with Annie McDonald)
- *Winners* (OUP 2010 – co-authored with Cathy Lawday)
- *New Ways to Go* (CUP 2002 – co-authored with Penny Ur and Ramon Ribé)

Acknowledgements

My first book, **Pronunciation Games**, was published back in 1995 by *CUP*. It was a photocopiable book of games with accompanying teachers' notes, designed by my sister Amanda Hancock. It seems appropriate that all these years later, my first ebooks **PronPack 1-4** should also be pronunciation activities – but printable rather than photocopiable this time – and again beautifully designed and produced by Amanda.

A huge thank you is also due to Annie McDonald for her editorial work and tireless encouragement, and to Henry Wong of Heliographic for his graphic design input.

I would also like to thank my students at *English in Chester* (www. english-in-chester.co.uk), who were the first to try out the activities in this book, and colleagues at that school who also trialled the material, especially Patsy Tyrer.

Last but not least I would like to thank my team of consultants/ reviewers around the globe, including:

Freya Barua *(India)*
Marina Cantarutti *(Argentina)*
Ariel Donnell-Clark *(UK)*
Cristina Gómez Martínez *(Spain)*
Ewa Grzelak *(Poland)*
Louise Guyett de Orozco *(Ireland)*
Oksana Hera *(Ukraine)*
Stella Maris Palavecino *(Argentina)*
José Mompean *(Spain)*
Lalitha Murthy *(India)*
Catarina Pontes *(Brazil)*
Jane Neill *(UK)*
Adam Scott *(UK)*
Elena Velikaya *(Russia)*

Editor: Annie McDonald
Book design: Amanda Hancock
Graphics: Heliographic
Illustration: Mark Hancock
Images: Shutterstock.com
Audio: Mark Hancock with Annie McDonald

For more information visit **www.pronpack.com**

Notes